Garden of the Heart

Selected Prayers for
Comfort and Strength

Garden

of the

Heart

Garden of the Heart
Selected Prayers for Comfort and Strength
©2022 Patricia Harmsen

Artwork by Patty Harmsen
Book design by Craig Harmsen
Dedicated to our parents and children

www.etsy.com/shop/pattysgardenstudio

First Edition 2022
ISBN 9780578356365
Printed in the USA

Contents

O YE DWELLERS IN THE HIGHEST PARADISE!

Proclaim unto the children of assurance that within the realms of holiness, nigh unto the celestial paradise, a new garden hath appeared, round which circle the denizens of the realm on high and the immortal dwellers of the exalted paradise. Strive, then, that ye may attain that station, that ye may unravel the mysteries of love from its windflowers and learn the secret of divine and consummate wisdom from its eternal fruits. Solaced are the eyes of them that enter and abide therein!

The Hidden Words
of Bahá'u'lláh

Prayers for
Spiritual Strength

He is the Compassionate, the All-Bountiful! O God, my God! Thou seest me, Thou knowest me; Thou art my Haven and my Refuge. None have I sought nor any will I seek save Thee; no path have I trodden nor any will I tread but the path of Thy love. In the darksome night of despair, my eye turneth expectant and full of hope to the morn of Thy boundless favor and at the hour of dawn my drooping soul is refreshed and strengthened in remembrance of Thy beauty and perfection. He whom the grace of Thy mercy aideth, though he be but a drop, shall become the boundless ocean, and the merest atom which the outpouring of Thy loving-kindness assisteth, shall shine even as the radiant star.

Shelter under Thy protection, O Thou Spirit of purity, Thou Who art the All-Bountiful Provider, this enthralled, enkindled servant of Thine. Aid him in this world of being to remain steadfast and firm in Thy love and grant that this broken-winged bird attain a refuge and shelter in Thy divine nest that abideth upon the celestial tree.

—'Abdu'l-Bahá

O Thou beloved of my heart and soul! I have no refuge save Thee. I raise no voice at dawn save in Thy commemoration and praise. Thy love encompasseth me and Thy grace is perfect. My hope is in Thee.

O God, give me a new life at every instant and bestow upon me the breaths of the Holy Spirit at every moment, in order that I may remain steadfast in Thy love, attain unto great felicity, perceive the manifest light and be in the state of utmost tranquillity and submissiveness.

Verily, Thou art the Giver, the Forgiver, the Compassionate.

—'Abdu'l-Bahá

O my Lord, my Beloved, my Desire! Befriend me in my loneliness and accompany me in my exile. Remove my sorrow. Cause me to be devoted to Thy beauty. Withdraw me from all else save Thee. Attract me through Thy fragrances of holiness. Cause me to be associated in Thy Kingdom with those who are severed from all else save Thee, who long to serve Thy sacred threshold and who stand to work in Thy Cause. Enable me to be one of Thy maidservants who have attained to Thy good pleasure. Verily, Thou art the Gracious, the Generous.

—'Abdu'l-Bahá

O Divine Providence! Perplexing difficulties have arisen and formidable obstacles have appeared. O Lord! Remove these difficulties and show forth the evidences of Thy might and power. Ease these hardships and smooth our way along this arduous path. O Divine Providence! The obstacles are unyielding, and our toil and hardship are conjoined with a myriad adversities. There is no helper save Thee, and no succourer except Thyself. We set all our hopes on Thee, and commit all our affairs unto Thy care. Thou art the Guide and the Remover of every difficulty, and Thou art the Wise, the Seeing, and the Hearing.

—'Abdu'l-Bahá

O Lord! Grant me a measure of Thy grace and loving-kindness, Thy care and protection, Thy shelter and bounty, that the end of my days may be distinguished above their beginning, and the close of my life may open the portals to Thy manifold blessings. May Thy loving-kindness and bounty descend upon me at every moment, and Thy forgiveness and mercy be vouchsafed with every breath, until, beneath the sheltering shadow of Thine upraised Standard, I may at last repair to the Kingdom of the All-Praised. Thou art the Bestower and the Ever-Loving, and Thou art, verily, the Lord of grace and bounty.

—'Abdu'l-Bahá

Thy name is my healing, O my God, and remembrance of Thee is my remedy. Nearness to Thee is my hope, and love for Thee is my companion. Thy mercy to me is my healing and my succor in both this world and the world to come. Thou, verily, art the All-Bountiful, the All-Knowing, the All-Wise.

—*Bahá'u'lláh*

Create in me a pure heart, O my God, and renew a tranquil conscience within me, O my Hope! Through the spirit of power confirm Thou me in Thy Cause, O my Best-Beloved, and by the light of Thy glory reveal unto me Thy path, O Thou the Goal of my desire! Through the power of Thy transcendent might lift me up unto the heaven of Thy holiness, O Source of my being, and by the breezes of Thine eternity gladden me, O Thou Who art my God! Let Thine everlasting melodies breathe tranquillity on me, O my Companion, and let the riches of Thine ancient countenance deliver me from all except Thee, O my Master, and let the tidings of the revelation of Thine incorruptible Essence bring me joy, O Thou Who art the most manifest of the manifest and the most hidden of the hidden!

—*Bahá'u'lláh*

O compassionate God! Thanks be to Thee for Thou hast awakened and made me conscious. Thou hast given me a seeing eye and favored me with a hearing ear, hast led me to Thy kingdom and guided me to Thy path. Thou hast shown me the right way and caused me to enter the ark of deliverance. O God! Keep me steadfast and make me firm and staunch. Protect me from violent tests and preserve and shelter me in the strongly fortified fortress of Thy Covenant and Testament. Thou art the Powerful. Thou art the Seeing. Thou art the Hearing.

O Thou the Compassionate God. Bestow upon me a heart which, like unto a glass, may be illumined with the light of Thy love, and confer upon me thoughts which may change this world into a rose garden through the outpourings of heavenly grace.

Thou art the Compassionate, the Merciful. Thou art the Great Beneficent God.

—'Abdu'l-Bahá

19

O God, my God! Give me to drink from the cup of Thy bestowal and illumine my face with the light of guidance. Make me firm in the path of faithfulness, assist me to be steadfast in Thy mighty Covenant, and suffer me to be numbered with Thy chosen servants. Unlock before my face the doors of abundance, grant me deliverance, and sustain me, through means I cannot reckon, from the treasuries of heaven. Suffer me to turn my face toward the countenance of Thy generosity and to be entirely devoted to Thee, O Thou Who art merciful and compassionate! To those that stand fast and firm in Thy Covenant Thou, verily, art gracious and generous. All praise be to God, the Lord of the worlds!

—'Abdu'l-Bahá

Prayers for Loved Ones

O Lord! Guard Thou the children that are born in Thy day, are nurtured at the breast of Thy love, and fostered in the bosom of Thy grace.

O Lord, they are verily young branches growing in the gardens of Thy knowledge, they are boughs budding in Thy groves of grace. Grant them a share of Thy generous gifts, make them to thrive and flourish in the rain that raineth from the clouds of Thy bestowal.

Thou art verily the Generous, the Clement, the Compassionate!

—ʻAbduʼl-Bahá

O Thou kind Lord! Bestow heavenly confirmation upon this daughter of the kingdom, and graciously aid her that she may remain firm and steadfast in Thy Cause and that she may, even as a nightingale of the rose garden of mysteries, warble melodies in the Abhá Kingdom in the most wondrous tones, thereby bringing happiness to everyone. Make her exalted among the daughters of the kingdom and enable her to attain life eternal.

Thou art the Bestower, the All-Loving.

—'Abdu'l-Bahá

O Lord! Plant this tender seedling in the garden of Thy manifold bounties, water it from the fountains of Thy loving-kindness and grant that it may grow into a goodly plant through the outpourings of Thy favour and grace.

Thou art the Mighty and the Powerful.

—'Abdu'l-Bahá

O Thou forgiving God! Forgive the sins of my loving mother, pardon her shortcomings, cast upon her the glance of Thy gracious providence, and enable her to gain admittance into Thy Kingdom.

O God! From the earliest days of my life she educated and nurtured me, yet I did not recompense her for her toil and labours. Do Thou reward her by granting her eternal life and making her exalted in Thy Kingdom.

Verily, Thou art the Forgiver, the Bestower, and the Kind.

—'Abdu'l-Bahá

He is God!

O peerless Lord! Praised be Thou for having kindled that light in the glass of the Concourse on high, for having guided that bird of faithfulness to the nest of the Abhá Kingdom. Thou hast joined that precious river to the mighty sea, Thou hast returned that spreading ray of light to the Sun of Truth. Thou hast welcomed that captive of remoteness into the garden of reunion, and led him who longed to look upon Thee to Thy presence in Thy bright place of lights.

Thou art the Lord of tender love, Thou art the last goal of the yearning heart, Thou art the dearest wish of the martyr's soul.

—'Abdu'l-Bahá

O Divine Providence! Immerse the father and mother of this servant of Thy Threshold in the ocean of Thy forgiveness, and purge and sanctify them from every sin and transgression. Grant them Thy forgiveness and mercy, and bestow upon them Thy gracious pardon. Thou, verily, art the Pardoner, the Ever-Forgiving, the Bestower of abundant grace. O Thou forgiving Lord! Though we are sinners, yet our hopes are fixed upon Thy promise and assurance. Though we are enveloped by the darkness of error, yet we have at all times turned our faces to the morn of Thy bountiful favours. Deal with us as beseemeth Thy Threshold, and confer upon us that which is worthy of Thy Court. Thou art the Ever-Forgiving, the Pardoner, He Who overlooketh every shortcoming.

—'Abdu'l-Bahá

O my Lord, O my Lord! These two bright orbs are wedded in Thy love, conjoined in servitude to Thy Holy Threshold, united in ministering to Thy Cause. Make Thou this marriage to be as threading lights of Thine abounding grace, O my Lord, the All-Merciful, and luminous rays of Thy bestowals, O Thou the Beneficent, the Ever-Giving, that there may branch out from this great tree boughs that will grow green and flourishing through the gifts that rain down from Thy clouds of grace.

Verily, Thou art the Generous. Verily, Thou art the Almighty. Verily, Thou art the Compassionate, the All-Merciful.

—'Abdu'l-Bahá

He is the All-Glorious.

O my Lord, my King, my Ruler, and my Sovereign! I call upon Thee with my tongue, my heart, and my soul, saying: Clothe this servant of Thine with the robe of Thy care, the raiment of Thine unfailing help, and the armour of Thy protection. Assist him to make mention of Thee and to extol Thy virtues amidst Thy people, and unloose his tongue to utter Thy glorification and praise in every assemblage held to celebrate Thy unity and sanctity. Thou art, in truth, the Mighty, the Powerful, the All-Glorious, the Self-Subsisting.

—'Abdu'l-Bahá

I beg Thy forgiveness, O my God, and implore pardon after the manner Thou wishest Thy servants to direct themselves to Thee. I beg of Thee to wash away our sins as befitteth Thy Lordship, and to forgive me, my parents, and those who in Thy estimation have entered the abode of Thy love in a manner which is worthy of Thy transcendent sovereignty and well beseemeth the glory of Thy celestial power.

O my God! Thou hast inspired my soul to offer its supplication to Thee, and but for Thee, I would not call upon Thee. Lauded and glorified art Thou; I yield Thee praise inasmuch as Thou didst reveal Thyself unto me, and I beg Thee to forgive me, since I have fallen short in my duty to know Thee and have failed to walk in the path of Thy love.

—*The Báb*

Prayers for Unity

O my God! O my God! Unite the hearts of Thy servants, and reveal to them Thy great purpose. May they follow Thy commandments and abide in Thy law. Help them, O God, in their endeavor, and grant them strength to serve Thee. O God! Leave them not to themselves, but guide their steps by the light of Thy knowledge, and cheer their hearts by Thy love. Verily, Thou art their Helper and their Lord.

—*Bahá'u'lláh*

O Thou Omnipotent Lord! We are all held within the mighty grasp of Thy power. Thou art our Supporter and our Helper. Grant us Thy tender mercy, bestow upon us Thy bounty, open the portals of grace, and cast upon us the glance of Thy favours. Let a vivifying breeze waft over us, and quicken Thou our yearning hearts. Illumine our eyes and make the sanctuary of our hearts the envy of every blossoming bower. Rejoice every soul and gladden every spirit. Reveal Thine ancient power and make manifest Thy great might. Cause the birds of human souls to soar to new heights, and let Thy confidants in this nether world fathom the mysteries of Thy Kingdom. Set firm our steps and bestow upon us unwavering hearts. We are sinners, and Thou art the Ever-Forgiving. We are Thy servants, and Thou art the Sovereign Lord. We are homeless wanderers, and Thou art our haven and refuge. Graciously aid and assist us to diffuse Thy sweet savours and to exalt Thy Word. Elevate the station of the dispossessed, and bestow Thine inexhaustible treasure upon the destitute. Vouchsafe Thy strength unto the weak, and confer heavenly power upon the feeble. Thou art the Provider, Thou art the Gracious, Thou art the Lord Who ruleth over all things.

—'Abdu'l-Bahá

O Thou peerless and loving Lord! Though capacity and worthiness are lacking, and it is infinitely hard to withstand tribulations, yet worthiness and capacity are gifts vouchsafed by Thee. O Lord! Give us capacity and make us worthy, that we may evince the most great steadfastness, renounce this world and all its people, kindle the fire of Thy love, and even as candles, burn bright with a consuming flame and shed abroad our radiance.

O Lord of the Kingdom! Deliver us from this world of vain illusions, and lead us unto the realm of the infinite. Suffer us to be wholly freed from this nether life, and cause us to be blessed with the bountiful gifts of the Kingdom. Release us from this world of nothingness that beareth the semblance of reality, and confer upon us life everlasting. Bestow on us joy and delight, and favour us with gladness and contentment. Comfort our hearts, and grant peace and tranquillity to our souls, so that upon ascending unto Thy Kingdom we may attain Thy presence and may rejoice in the realms above. Thou art the Giver, the Bestower, the Almighty!

—'Abdu'l-Bahá

O Thou Lord of wondrous grace!

Bestow upon us new blessings. Give to us the freshness of the spring. We are saplings which have been planted by the fingers of Thy bounty and have been formed out of the water and clay of Thy tender affection. We thirst for the living waters of Thy favours and are dependent upon the outpourings of the clouds of Thy generosity. Abandon not to itself this grove wherein our hopes aspire, nor withhold there-from the showers of Thy loving-kindness. Grant that from the clouds of Thy mercy may fall copious rain so that the trees of our lives may bring forth fruit and we may attain the most cherished desire of our hearts.

—'Abdu'l-Bahá

O Thou kind Lord! O Thou Who art generous and merciful! We are the servants of Thy threshold and are gathered beneath the sheltering shadow of Thy divine unity. The sun of Thy mercy is shining upon all, and the clouds of Thy bounty shower upon all. Thy gifts encompass all, Thy loving providence sustains all, Thy protection overshadows all, and the glances of Thy favor are cast upon all. O Lord! Grant Thine infinite bestowals, and let the light of Thy guidance shine. Illumine the eyes, gladden the hearts with abiding joy. Confer a new spirit upon all people and bestow upon them eternal life. Unlock the gates of true under-standing and let the light of faith shine resplendent. Gather all people beneath the shadow of Thy bounty and cause them to unite in harmony, so that they may become as the rays of one sun, as the waves of one ocean, and as the fruit of one tree. May they drink from the same fountain. May they be refreshed by the same breeze. May they receive illumination from the same source of light. Thou art the Giver, the Merciful, the Omnipotent.

—'Abdu'l-Bahá

O my kind Lord, O Thou the desire of my heart and soul! Bestow upon Thy friends Thy loving-kindness, and grant them Thine unfailing mercy. Be Thou a solace to Thine ardent lovers, and a friend, a comforter, and a loving companion to them who yearn for Thee. Their hearts are ablaze with the fire of Thy love, and their souls are consumed with the flame of devotion to Thee. They long, one and all, to hasten unto the altar of love, that they may willingly lay down their lives.

O Divine Providence! Grant them Thy favour, guide them aright, graciously aid them to achieve spiritual victory, and confer upon them heavenly bestowals. O Lord, assist them by Thy munificence and grace, and make their radiant faces lamps of guidance in assemblies devoted to the knowledge of Thee, and signs of heavenly bounty in gatherings where Thy verses are expounded. Thou art, verily, the Merciful, the All-Bountiful, the One Whose help is implored by all men.

—'Abdu'l-Bahá

O God, my God! Aid Thou Thy trusted servants to have loving and tender hearts. Help them to spread, amongst all the nations of the earth, the light of guidance that cometh from the Company on high. Verily, Thou art the Strong, the Powerful, the Mighty, the All-Subduing, the Ever-Giving. Verily, Thou art the Generous, the Gentle, the Tender, the Most Bountiful.

—*'Abdu'l-Bahá*

O Lord! What an outpouring of bounty Thou hast vouchsafed, and what a flood of abounding grace Thou hast granted! Thou didst make all the hearts to become even as a single heart, and all the souls to be bound together as one soul. Thou didst endow inert bodies with life and feeling, and didst bestow upon lifeless frames the consciousness of the spirit. Through the effulgent rays shed from the Day-Star of the All-Merciful, Thou didst invest these atoms of dust with visible existence, and through the billows of the ocean of oneness, Thou didst enable these evanescent drops to surge and roar.

O Almighty One Who endowest a blade of straw with the might of a mountain and enablest a speck of dust to mirror forth the glory of the resplendent sun! Grant us Thy tender grace and favour, so that we may arise to serve Thy Cause and not be shamefaced before the peoples of the earth.

—'Abdu'l-Bahá

O thou who art turning thy face towards God! Close thine eyes to all things else, and open them to the realm of the All-Glorious. Ask whatsoever thou wishest of Him alone; seek whatsoever thou seekest from Him alone. With a look He granteth a hundred thousand hopes, with a glance He healeth a hundred thousand incurable ills, with a nod He layeth balm on every wound, with a glimpse He freeth the hearts from the shackles of grief. He doeth as He doeth, and what recourse have we? He carrieth out His Will, He ordaineth what He pleaseth. Then better for thee to bow down thy head in submission, and put thy trust in the All-Merciful Lord.

Selections from the
Writings of 'Abdu'l-Bahá

Bibliography

1. Bahá'u'lláh. The Hidden Words (Bahá'í Reference Library, https://
www.bahai.org/library/), From the Persian, 18.

5. Bahá'u'lláh. Bahá'í Prayers (Bahá'í Reference Library), Prayers/General
Prayers/Nearness to God.

7. 'Abdu'l-Bahá. Additional Prayers Revealed by 'Abdu'l-Bahá (Bahá'í
Reference Library), O Thou beloved of my heart and soul! I have no refuge
save Thee. I raise...

9. 'Abdu'l-Bahá. Bahá'í Prayers (Baha'i Reference Library), Prayers/General
Prayers/Women.

11. 'Abdu'l-Bahá. Prayers of 'Abdu'l-Bahá (Bahá'í Reference Library), 6.

13. 'Abdu'l-Bahá. Prayers of 'Abdu'l-Bahá (Bahá'í Reference Library), 10.

15. Bahá'u'lláh. Prayers and Meditations by Bahá'u'lláh, (Bahá'í Reference
Library), CLXX.

17. Bahá'u'lláh. Bahá'í Prayers (Bahá'í Reference Library), Prayers/General
Prayers/Spiritual Growth.

19. 'Abdu'l-Bahá. Bahá'í Prayers (Bahá'í Reference Library), Prayers/
General Prayers/Firmness in the Covenant.

21. 'Abdu'l-Bahá. Additional Prayers Revealed by 'Abdu'l-Bahá (Bahá'í
Reference Library), O God, my God! Give me to drink from the cup of Thy
bestowal and illumine my face...

25. 'Abdu'l-Bahá. Bahá'í Prayers and Tablets for Children (Bahá'í
Reference Library), 17.

27. 'Abdu'l-Bahá. Bahá'í Prayers (Bahá'í Reference Library), Prayers/
General Prayers/Youth

29. 'Abdu'l-Bahá. Bahá'í Prayers and Tablets for Children (Bahá'í
Reference Library), 10.

31. 'Abdu'l-Bahá. Additional Prayers Revealed by 'Abdu'l-Bahá (Bahá'í Reference Library), O Thou forgiving God! Forgive the sins of my loving mother, pardon her shortcomings...

33. 'Abdu'l-Bahá. Additional Prayers Revealed by 'Abdu'l-Bahá (Bahá'í Reference Library), O peerless Lord! Praised be Thou for having kindled that light in the glass of the Concourse on high...

35. 'Abdu'l-Bahá. Prayers of 'Abdu'l-Bahá (Bahá'í Reference Library), 13.

37. 'Abdu'l-Bahá. Bahá'í Prayers (Bahá'í Reference Library), Prayers/General Prayers/Marriage.

39. 'Abdu'l-Bahá. Prayers of 'Abdu'l-Bahá (Bahá'í Reference Library), 20.

41. The Báb. Bahá'í Prayers (Bahá'í Reference Library), Prayers/General Prayers/Families.

45. Bahá'u'lláh. Bahá'í Prayers (Bahá'í Reference Library), Prayers/General Prayers/Families.

47. 'Abdu'l-Bahá. Prayers of 'Abdu'l-Bahá (Bahá'í Reference Library), 16.

49. 'Abdu'l-Bahá. Prayers of 'Abdu'l-Bahá (Bahá'í Reference Library), 3.

51. 'Abdu'l-Bahá. Bahá'í Prayers and Tablets for Children (Bahá'í Reference Library), 37.

53. 'Abdu'l-Bahá, Bahá'í Prayers (Bahá'í Reference Library), Prayers/General Prayers/Humanity.

55. 'Abdu'l-Bahá. Prayers of 'Abdu'l-Bahá (Bahá'í Reference Library), 21.

57. 'Abdu'l-Bahá. Bahá'í Prayers (Bahá'í Reference Library), Prayers/General Prayers/Teaching.

59. 'Abdu'l-Bahá. Prayers of 'Abdu'l-Bahá (Bahá'í Reference Library), 15.

60. 'Abdu'l-Bahá, Selections from the Writings of 'Abdu'l-Bahá (Baha'i Reference Library), p. 51.

Made in United States
North Haven, CT
26 December 2023